FIRST FACTS

The Sea

Kingfisher

NEW YORK

Author
Nina Morgan

Natural history consultant
Michael Chinery

Educational consultant
Daphne Ingram

Series consultant
Brian Williams

Editor
Camilla Hallinan

Designer
Tony Potter, Times Four Publishing

Illustrators
John Barber (pages 12-13, 16-17, 18-19, 22-23,
26-29 & 40)
Bob Corley (30-31, 38-39, 46-47, 50-53 & 62-63)
Peter Dennis (15, 43, 72, 92-102 & 106-119)
Terry Hadler (17, 22, 42 & 44-47)
David Kearney (103)
Swanston Graphics (12, 14-15, 18-19, 22-25, 40-41,
86-87 & 118-19)
Treve Tamblin (32-35, 54-61, 64-67 & 70-89)

About this book

Have you ever stood on the beach and wondered how big the sea is? If you were out in space and you looked down at the Earth, you would see that seas and oceans cover most of our planet. This book shows how important they are.

The sea helps to control the world's climate. It also helps to shape the coastline, whether there is a towering cliff or a flat, soggy marsh. The sea provides a home for millions of plants and animals. It is also full of valuable resources—food, oil, salt, and many other things we use every day.

From the tiny grains of sand on the beach to the dramatic mountains and valleys hidden deep beneath the water, the sea is a fascinating place. But people are damaging the sea, and it needs your help. With this book, you can begin to find out more about the sea. Only by finding out more can we all learn how to use the sea more wisely.

Nina Morgan

CONTENTS

OCEAN RICHES

PEOPLE AND THE SEA

World of

water

Our blue planet

If you looked down at the Earth from space, you would see that most of our planet is covered by the ocean.

More than 70 percent of the Earth is covered in water.

Life began in the ocean about 3,500 million years ago. Tiny plants produced a gas called oxygen. Oxygen made it possible for other forms of life to develop.

plankton

Now the ocean is home to millions of plants and animals—from tiny plankton to huge blue whales.

Oceans and seas

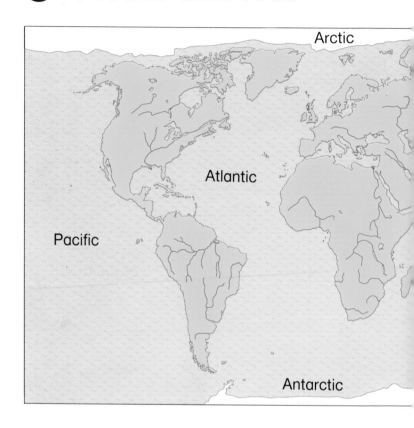

There is really only one ocean on the Earth. This huge ocean is separated into five smaller oceans by the continents. The five oceans are the Pacific, Atlantic, Indian, Arctic, and Antarctic Oceans.

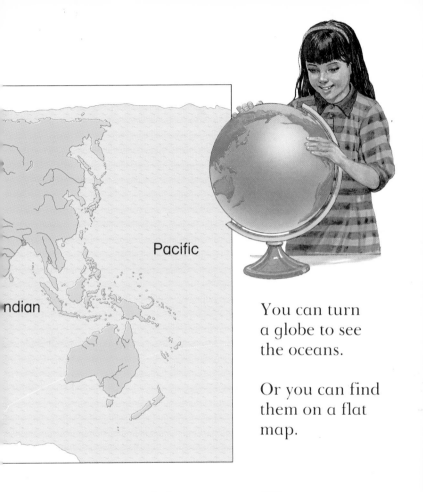

Pacific

Indian

You can turn a globe to see the oceans.

Or you can find them on a flat map.

Seas are parts of the oceans. The Mediterranean, the Bering Sea, and the Caribbean are the largest seas, but there are also many others. (Sometimes people say "sea" when they mean "ocean.")

15

🌐 Seawater

If you have ever swum in the sea and tasted seawater, you will know that it is salty. Seawater is salty because it contains salts and minerals from rocks.

fresh water

seawater

Some salts and minerals are dissolved from rocks on the seafloor. Others are carried into the sea from rocks on land, by streams and rivers. River water does not taste salty. It is called fresh water.

Salt helps you float when you swim in the sea. Some parts of the oceans are very salty. The saltiest water is in the Dead Sea between Israel and Jordan. But it is not a sea at all. It is a lake.

The least salty part of the oceans is in the Atlantic Ocean, off South America. There, the Amazon River pours millions of gallons of fresh water into the ocean.

🌐 Warm water, cold water

Sunlight heats the water near the surface of the sea.

In the tropics around the equator, the sun shines for many hours each day. So the sea is warm enough to swim in all the year round.

Less sunlight shines on the oceans around the North and South poles.

South Pole

In the Arctic and Antarctic Oceans around the poles, the water is so cold that it freezes. The huge pieces of floating ice are called ice floes or ice packs.

polar sea

North Pole

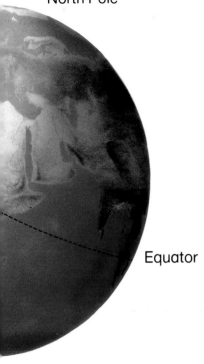

Equator

All seawater is cold deep down. Cold water is heavier than warm water, so it sinks to the bottom. Sunlight cannot reach that far down.

tropical sea

19

Amazing facts

Ninety-seven percent of all the water on the Earth is in the oceans.

The Pacific is the biggest ocean, and the deepest. The Arctic is the smallest ocean, and the shallowest.

The coldest sea surface temperature is 28 degrees Fahrenheit. That is in the White Sea, in the Arctic Ocean.

The warmest sea surface temperature is 96 degrees Fahrenheit. This occurs in the summer, in shallow parts of the Persian Gulf in the Indian Ocean.

Some ice floes are so big that people live on them. Russian scientists once built a research station on a huge ice floe in the Antarctic. After several years they had to leave because the ice began to melt.

A changing

world

The changing world

The surface of the Earth is a thin shell of rock called the crust. The crust is made up of 13 huge pieces called plates.

Hot, soft rock flows up from inside the Earth and pushes these plates around. This movement is called plate tectonics.

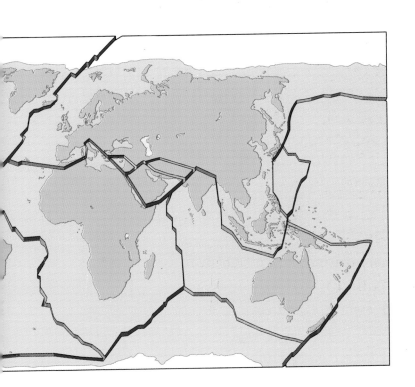

Some parts of the Earth's surface move
as much as 8 inches every year.
The movement of the plates means
the continents and oceans are
slowly changing shape
all the time.

The story of the oceans

200 million years ago

Two hundred million years ago, there was only one continent, called Pangaea (pan-gee-ah).

Pangaea was surrounded by a single ocean.

Currents of hot soft rock came up from inside the Earth. Little by little, they opened up large cracks in the land. Pieces of Pangaea split off and drifted apart to form new continents.

65 million years ago

Molten or liquid rock welled up and formed new seafloor in the gaps. Water flowed in and formed new oceans.

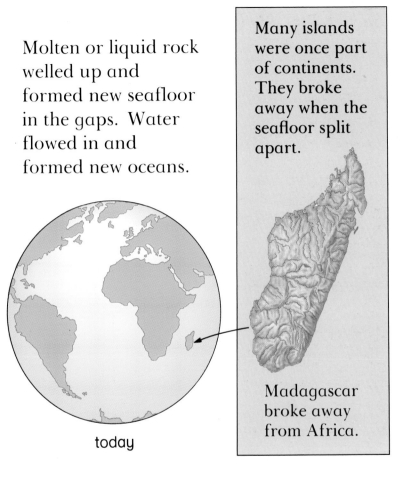

Many islands were once part of continents. They broke away when the seafloor split apart.

Madagascar broke away from Africa.

today

The size and shape of the oceans are still changing. The Atlantic Ocean is growing about 1½ inches wider every year. The Pacific Ocean is becoming narrower.

The ocean floor

At the edge of each continent, the land forms a shallow shelf under the sea. The edge of the shelf slopes steeply down to the seafloor. The large flat areas on the seafloor are called abyssal plains.

But the seafloor is not flat everywhere.

In some places, the seafloor is covered with small extinct volcanoes called abyssal hills. There are also towering mountains called seamounts—they were made by large volcanoes. And there are deep gorges called trenches. Underwater landscape is as dramatic as the Grand Canyon!

In the trench

Trenches are deep, narrow valleys. It is pitch dark in the trenches because sunlight cannot reach the bottom. Most trenches are in the Pacific Ocean. The deepest is the Marianas Trench, near Japan.

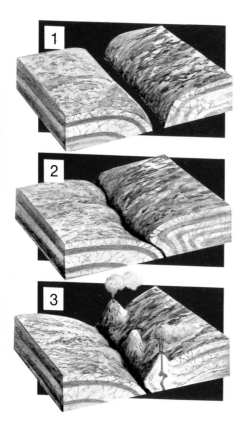

When two plates in the Earth's crust collide, one plate is pushed below the other. The gap between them forms a trench. This takes thousands of years.

Both plates are under pressure. So earthquakes and volcanic eruptions occur.

The Marianas Trench is 7 miles deep. If you dropped Mount Everest in the trench, the mountain's peak would not reach the surface.

surface

Mount Everest

one
mile
deep

seven
miles
deep

Underwater mountains

The longest mountain chains on Earth are underwater. They are called the mid-ocean ridges. This is how they form.

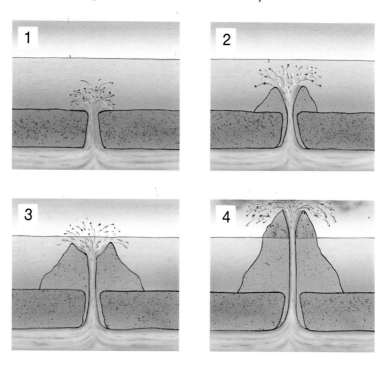

When plates move apart, molten rock wells up. It hardens into ridges. As more molten rock wells up, the ridges grow higher.

Some parts of the ridges poke through the ocean surface and make new islands.

New islands are also formed when underwater volcanoes erupt.

After each eruption, volcanic lava forms a new layer of rock. Eventually the volcano grows tall enough to reach the surface.

Coral islands

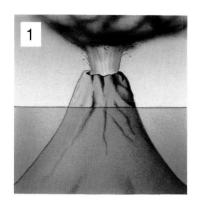

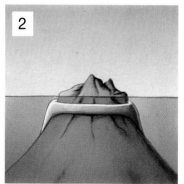

When an island emerges in warm parts of the world, tiny animals called corals may come to live in the warm, shallow water around the island. The corals build a reef on the sides of the island. The reef is home to masses of colorful plants and animals.

Over thousands of years, the island may begin to sink. The corals build upward, to stay in warm, shallow water. After the island sinks below the surface, all that can be seen above is a ring of coral reef called an atoll. The water inside the atoll forms a lagoon.

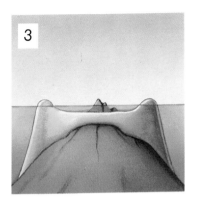

3

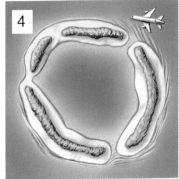

4

On the reef

It takes millions of corals to build a reef. Even a small piece of coral is made of hundreds of tiny animals. They start life as buds growing on their parents. Each animal has a hard limestone shell.

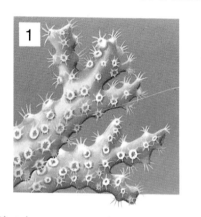

sea fan

mushroom coral

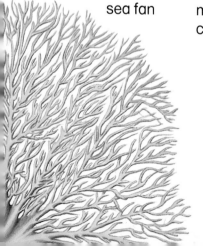

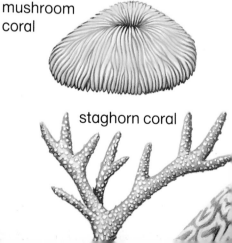

staghorn coral

When corals die, new corals build on top of their shells. The layers of coral form walls of limestone. These walls are the reefs.

Many types of animals and plants live in and around coral reefs, because they can find a safe place to live and plenty to eat.

orange
cup coral

brain coral

The crown-of-thorns starfish eats coral. These animals can kill a coral reef in just a few months.

Amazing facts

The highest underwater mountain is in the Pacific, between Samoa and New Zealand. It is 5.4 miles high. That is nearly as tall as Mount Everest, the world's highest mountain.

Iceland is made up of the tops of some of the volcanoes in the mid-Atlantic ridge.

Greenland is the largest island. It was once part of the North American continent.

One of the newest islands is Lateika, in the Pacific. This island was formed when a volcano erupted in the 1970s.

The longest coral reef is the Great Barrier Reef, in the Pacific. This stretches for over 1,200 miles along the north-eastern coast of Australia.

Wind and

waves

≋ Oceans and weather

The oceans help to control the climate. They do this by soaking up heat from the Sun during the day, and by releasing it very slowly at night.

The oceans are also an important part of the water cycle.

In the cycle, the Sun's heat turns some seawater into an invisible gas called water vapor. The vapor rises into the air. When it reaches cold air, the vapor turns into tiny drops of water.

The drops of water join together and make clouds. The water in the clouds falls as rain, snow, or hail. Most of it falls into the oceans. But even when it falls on land, the water eventually flows back into the oceans.

≋ Ocean currents

Currents are like huge rivers in the ocean. They carry water from one part of the world to another. Some currents flow near the surface. Icebergs drift on surface currents around the poles. Other currents flow deep down, along the seafloor.

There are many surface currents. Some are warm and some are cold. They link up and make six large loops called gyres.

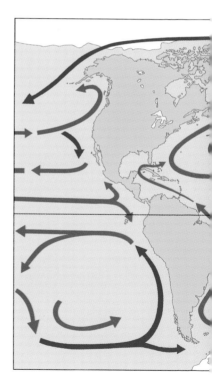

Strong winds in the tropics around the equator push the surface currents from east to west. Near the poles, winds push the currents back round again.

As the winds push them along, the currents bend around the continents and change direction.

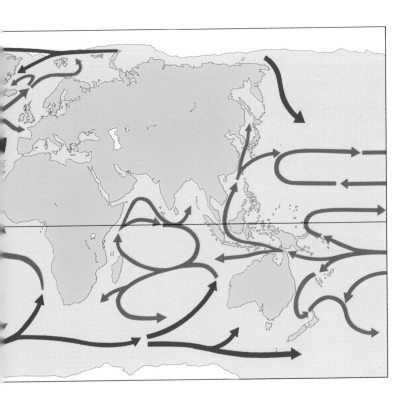

 # Waves

Waves are made by wind blowing across the ocean. Water in the waves seems to move forward, but really the water moves up and around and down.

The top of the wave is called the crest, and the bottom is called the trough.

When waves reach the shore they break. Waves break because water at the bottom catches on the seabed, while water on the crest keeps moving forward.

wind crest

trough

Surfers like high waves. These occur when strong winds blow for days across wide stretches of ocean. The highest waves are found in the biggest ocean, the Pacific.

42

≈ Stormy seas

In a storm, strong winds blow across the surface of the sea. As the winds blow, they whip up huge waves with ragged foamy edges. This kind of wave is called a whitecap. In really violent storms, whitecaps can be more than 50 feet high.

The most dangerous waves are tsunamis. These waves are started by underwater earthquakes and volcanic eruptions. Out at sea, tsunamis are low. But when a tsunami reaches land, it rears up to a huge height and crashes down with great force. A tsunami can cause terrible damage.

45

≋ The tides

Moon

Earth

high tide

low tide

Twice a day, tides make the oceans' water
level rise and fall. During a high tide, the
water moves farther onto the land. During
a low tide, the water moves back.

What causes tides? The Moon's pull, and
the Earth's spin.

On the side of the globe facing the Moon, the Moon's gravity pulls the oceans.

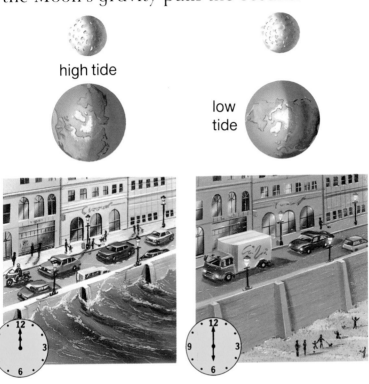

high tide

low tide

On the other side of the globe, the Moon's gravity pulls the Earth away from the oceans. So both places have high tides.

Every 24 hours the Earth spins right around. So most coasts have two high tides a day. Follow the red dot to see why.

Amazing facts

≈ The Gulf Stream is a current that brings warm water from the tropics all the way up the Atlantic to western Europe.

≈ The highest tsunami was 1,700 feet high. It started in the Pacific Ocean and hit land in Lituya Bay in Alaska, in 1958.

≈ The highest tides in the world occur in the Atlantic Ocean, in the Bay of Fundy in Canada. Here, the difference between low and high tides is more than 50 feet.

≈ Extra-high high tides tides occur when the Moon is between the Earth and the Sun. Then the Sun and the Moon both pull on the oceans. These tides are called spring tides.

Coastlines

Along the coast

Coastlines are where the land meets the sea. Some coastlines are formed as a result of erosion. Erosion takes place when wind and waves beat against the land and break it up.

Erosion goes on all the time, so the shape of a coastline is always changing.

Sometimes the waves wear away soft rock in the cliff. This forms a bay.
The harder rock may be left sticking out as a peninsula or headland. Sometimes part of the headland is worn right through to form stacks and arches.

And on some coastlines, waves carve out caves at the bottom of the cliffs.

🐚 Sand and pebbles

Sand is made by erosion. Waves wash over boulders of rock and rub them against one another. This slowly breaks them up.

The pieces of boulder are worn down into small pebbles, then gravel, and finally tiny grains of sand.

Beaches form where the waves drop sand and gravel and other sediment onto the shore. If the waves and currents are very strong, they carry away the sand and leave just the gravel, pebbles, or boulders.

Beach sediments are always on the move. Waves and currents move them along the coast or into deeper water.

Nesting in the cliffs

The coastline is home to many plants and animals.

Puffins, gannets, and guillemots all nest on cliffs. They live close to one another, but each has its own territory.

Puffins build their nests in burrows at the top of the cliff. Gannets make nests out of seaweed. Guillemots don't build nests at all. They simply lay their eggs on a rocky ledge.

These seabirds don't have to go far to find their food. The sea provides plenty of fish and plankton to eat. The birds use rising currents of warm air to soar up from the water and back to their nesting sites.

🐚 The water's edge

Animals and plants that live on a rocky shore lead a double life. When the tide is in, they must live underwater. When the tide is out, they must survive in the air.

Barnacles and mussels live on the rocks. When the tide is in, these animals open their shells and stick out their feathery legs to catch plankton. Plankton are too small to see, but the water is full of them.

Snails and limpets come out of their shells and graze on the seaweed growing on the rocks. Starfish feed on the snails and the mussels. Crabs hunt for food too—they eat almost anything! Prawns, anemones, and small fish live in pools that do not dry up.

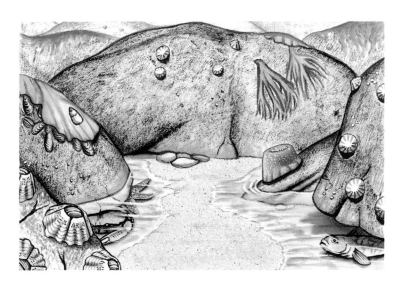

When the tide goes out, the snails and limpets cling to the rocks. Barnacles and mussels close their shells up tight. Crabs and starfish look for hiding places and wait for the next high tide.

 Seaweed

Seaweeds live along rocky shores.
These plants do not have roots because
there is no soil for them to dig into.
Instead, holdfasts at the base of their stems
grip tightly to the rocks.

Seaweeds bend with the water. So they
don't get damaged by the waves, tides, and
currents. Some have gas-filled swellings,
to keep them afloat in the water.

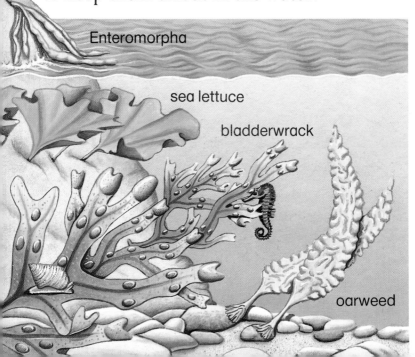

Enteromorpha

sea lettuce

bladderwrack

oarweed

Seaweeds live at different depths in the water. Sea lettuce lives in shallow water, where it is often exposed to air. Giant kelp forms dense forests in deep water.

Many animals live among the seaweeds. Snails and sea urchins graze seaweed for food. Some fish lay their eggs on seaweed, so they can hatch safely. Seals and sea otters hide in the kelp forests.

giant kelp

In the sand

On sandy shores, the wind often blows the sand into small hills called dunes. Grasses grow on the dunes and hold them in place.

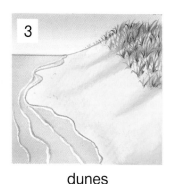

dunes

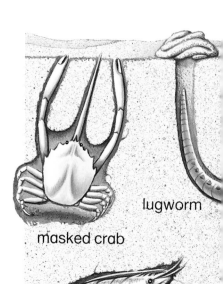

masked crab

lugworm

shrimp

Along the beach, animals burrow in the sand to protect themselves when the tide is out.

Some shellfish use a kind of foot to dig themselves into the sand. Razorshell clams have a large foot and a narrow shell, so they can bury themselves quickly. When the tide is in, these shellfish stick out tubes called siphons and suck in seawater. The water contains tiny bits of food.

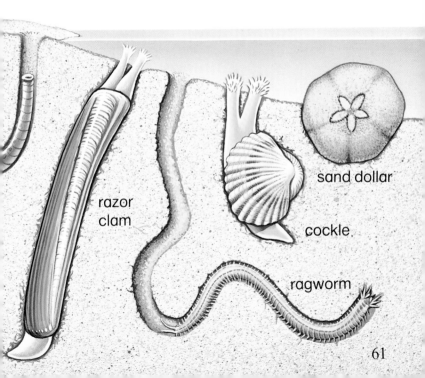

sand dollar

razor clam

cockle

ragworm

61

🐚 Estuaries and deltas

An estuary is the wide mouth of a river where it meets the sea. Some rivers carry huge amounts of sand and mud down to the shore and dump it there. So the shore builds out into the sea. This is called deposition.

When a river dumps sand and mud faster than the ocean carries it away, a delta forms.

A delta is low-lying land shaped a bit like a triangle. The top of the triangle starts at the river mouth. As the river dumps more sediment, the delta grows wider. The river has to divide into several channels to flow through the delta and reach the sea.

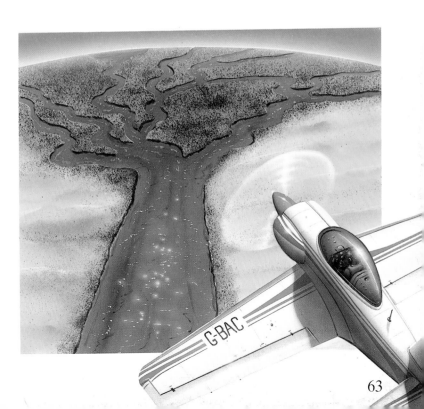

On the mudflats

In estuaries and deltas, the amount of salt in the water constantly changes. When the tide is in, the mudflats are flooded with salty seawater. When the tide is out, only fresh river water flows through.
The plants and animals here have to cope with both types of water.

curlew
oystercatcher

Birds use their beaks to poke into the mud to find worms and other animals that bury themselves in the mud.

It's easy to see why this bird is called a stilt!

With its long legs and long pointed beak, it can wade through the water and probe the mud for food.

stilt

redshank   turnstone

Some animals are buried deeper than others. Birds have beaks that are especially suited for finding the food they eat.

Marshes and swamps

Where land meets ocean, there are sometimes soggy pieces of land called marshes and swamps. Marshes have no trees. Swamps do.

In marshes the roots of grasses and other plants trap sediment and stop it being washed away by the sea.

Mangrove trees grow in tropical swamps. Their long roots arch high above the mud. Roots anchor the tree in the mud, and they keep the rest of the tree above water, even at high tide. The roots also help build up the coast, because they trap sediment.

Amazing facts

Some sand is made not of rock but of pieces of shells ground up by the waves.

On some coasts, 70 pairs of guillemots nest together in just one square yard. That's about the same amount of space as an armchair!

Sea urchins eat kelp. Sea otters feed on the urchins and protect the kelp from being destroyed.

The Mississippi Delta is growing out into the Gulf of Mexico at the rate of 300 feet every year.

Deltas were named after the letter d or delta in the Greek alphabet, because that letter is shaped like a triangle.

The open

sea

🐟 Ocean zones

There are four main depth zones in the ocean. Different types of animals live in each zone.

The shallowest zone is called the epipelagic zone. Sunlight warms the water in this zone, and many plants live here. So many animals live here too, because they feed on the plants.

The next zone is called the mesopelagic zone. Sunlight barely reaches this far down, so plants cannot grow here. The animals living here must swim up to the epipelagic zone at night to feed.

In the bathypelagic and the really deep abyssopelagic zones, it is pitch dark. Very few animals live here. They must work hard to find food. Some eat particles of food that drift down from above. Some are skillful hunters.

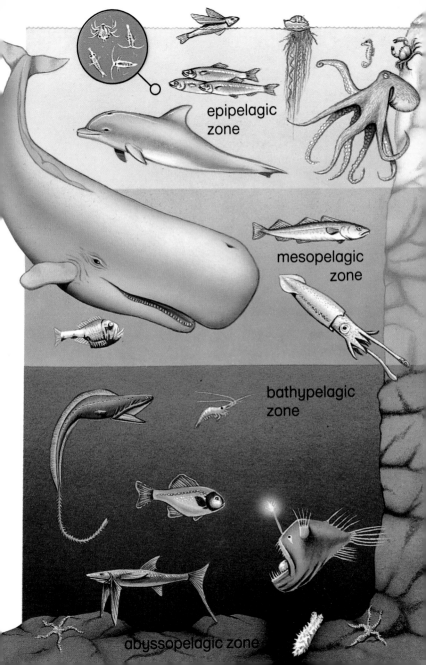

epipelagic zone

mesopelagic zone

bathypelagic zone

abyssopelagic zone

🐟 Plankton

The most important living things in the oceans are also the smallest. These are the plants and animals called plankton.

phytoplankton

zooplankton

Phytoplankton are plants. Zooplankton are animals.

Most plankton are so small that you can see them only with a microscope. There are millions of plankton in a jar of seawater.

sea anemone

Plankton are tiny, but they are food for many of the animals in the sea.

Sea anemones and corals on the seabed feed on plankton in shallow water.

jellyfish

Floating animals such as jellyfish feed on plankton. So do many fish such as mackerel.

mackerel

Blue whales, the largest animals in the ocean, feed on zooplankton called krill. One whale can eat four tons a day!

blue whale

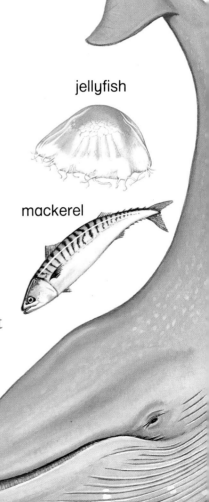

🐟 Ocean food

Imagine animals and plants in the sea as links in a chain. They all need food.

Plants are at the end of the chain. They use sunlight as their food. Next are the small animals that feed on plants. Then there are the animals that eat them.

After that, there is an even larger animal hunting for its food.

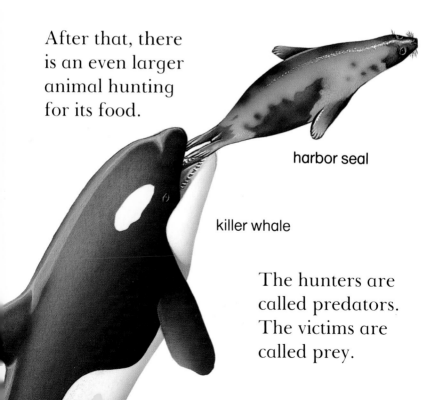

harbor seal

killer whale

The hunters are called predators. The victims are called prey.

Different animals feed on different things. So there are thousands of different food chains in the oceans. One is shown here.

phytoplankton

copepods

herring

cod

Nothing is wasted in the oceans. Animal droppings, and dead animals and plants, are broken down by tiny bacteria. This releases minerals. The minerals help to nourish the phytoplankton.

bacteria
(seen through a
powerful microscope)

🐟 Staying alive

To survive in the ocean an animal must find food, and it must avoid being eaten.

The octopus squirts a jet of dark ink to confuse predators. Then the octopus darts away and hides.

The sea dragon looks like a piece of seaweed. So it's hard to see.

Sea urchins protect themselves with spines that make them difficult to eat.

The Portuguese man-of-war has trailing tentacles up to 40 feet long.
Their sting can be as poisonous as a cobra bite.

The clown fish is safe among the stinging tentacles of sea anemones. It does not get stung—but predators do. The anemones get scraps from the fish's meals.

≈ Safety in numbers

Many sea creatures travel together in large groups called schools or shoals, to protect themselves.

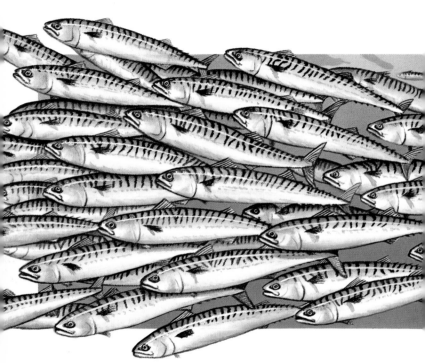

A huge school of fish confuses predators and makes it difficult for them to pick out just one to eat. But that is not enough to protect these mackerel from a barracuda.

Barracudas are often called "the tigers of the sea," because they are fierce hunters. The biggest barracudas are almost six feet long. They are fast swimmers.

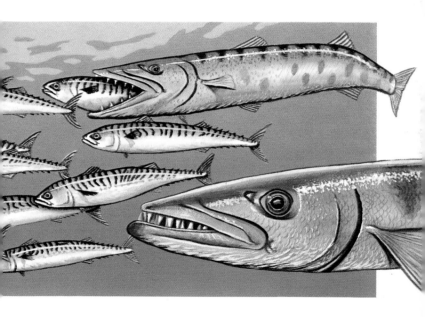

To catch their prey, barracudas race through schools of fish and attack them with snapping bites. You can see that a barracuda has a mouthful of sharp teeth.

A fish

There are about 13,000 different types, or species, of fish living in the oceans. This one is a goldfish.

Fish use their fins to help them swim through the water. The tail fin is waved from side to side to push the fish forward.

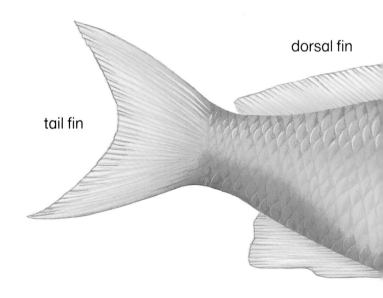

dorsal fin

tail fin

Other fins help the fish to stay upright and to change direction.

We breathe in oxygen from the air. Fish get their oxygen from the water.

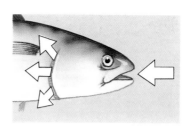

A fish has gills, hidden behind gill slits on either side of its head. Water comes in through the fish's mouth. The gills take in oxygen from the water. Then the water goes out through the gill slits.

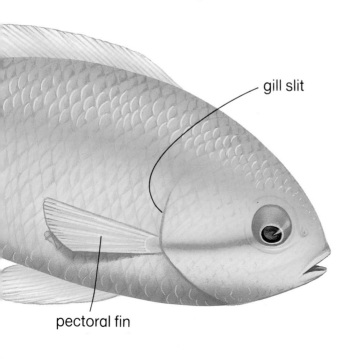

gill slit

pectoral fin

🐟 Ocean giants

Whales, dolphins, and porpoises are not
fish. They are mammals. Fish lay eggs.
But whales, dolphins, and porpoises give
birth to their babies and feed them with
their own milk—just as other mammals do.

Fish have gills to take oxygen from the
water. Whales, dolphins, and porpoises
have lungs, so they must rise to the surface
for air. They breathe in and out through a
blow-hole on the top of their heads.

blow-hole

Smaller whales, such as killer whales, have teeth. But the largest whales, including humpback whales, have no teeth.

Instead, they have thin strips of baleen. The whale takes a huge gulp of water, and strains it out again through the baleen. The baleen traps the plankton, like a giant sieve. Baleen whales eat tons of plankton a day.

🐟 Sea sounds

Below the surface the oceans are full of
noisy animals. Dolphins and whales give
off a series of clicks. These sounds bounce
back off other animals like an echo.

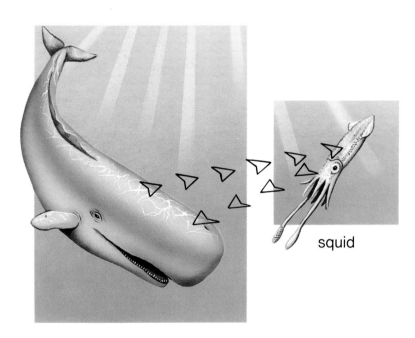

squid

The echoes help dolphins and whales to
find their prey. Sperm whales can find
squid up to 1,300 feet away.

Dolphins and whales also produce clicks and whistles and other sounds to communicate with one another.

Scientists record these sounds. But they do not understand whale language yet.

Humpback whales sing songs that last up to 20 minutes. But no one knows why.

⬤ Sea journeys

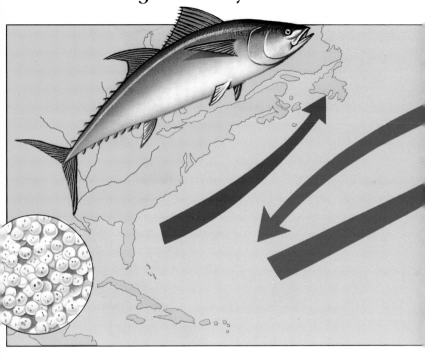

Many sea creatures regularly make long journeys. These are called migrations. Bluefin tuna lay their eggs in the warm waters of the Caribbean Sea. Then they migrate north across the Atlantic Ocean to Nova Scotia. On the way they find lots to eat, and nearly double their weight.

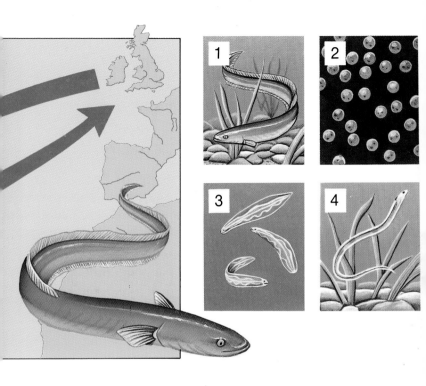

Some eels make an even longer journey.
They leave their rivers in Europe and swim
across the Atlantic Ocean to the Sargasso
Sea near Bermuda, to lay their eggs.
The eggs hatch and the young eels travel
in the Gulf Stream current all the way back
to the rivers in Europe.

In the dark

The deep ocean is very cold, no
warmer than 37 degrees Fahrenheit,
and very dark. There is not much
food, so few animals live here. Those
that do are often very small. They can
survive on little food. Some of them eat
only once every few months.

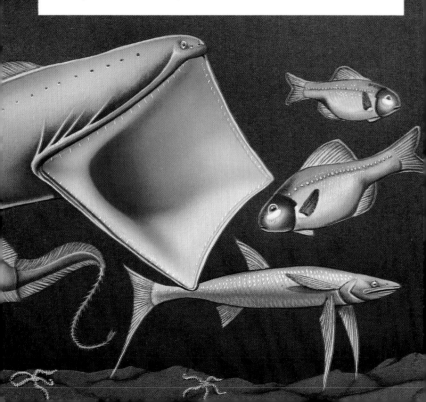

The gulper eel has jaws that open wide to gulp its prey. The angler fish waves a glowing lure to attract prey into its mouth. Flashlight fish light up parts of their bodies to signal to one another. Down on the seabed, tripod fish use their long fins like three stilts.

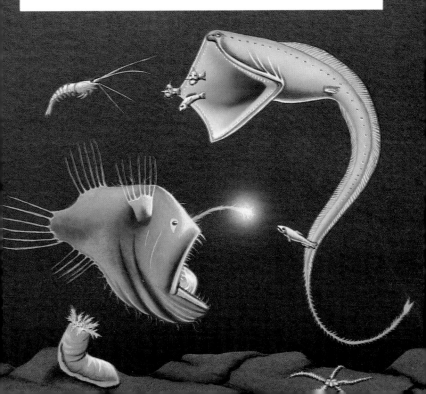

Amazing facts

The name plankton comes from the Greek word for wandering. Plankton cannot swim—they drift wherever the currents take them.

In an emergency most fish can swim ten times their body length in one second.

The stonefish which lives among coral reefs in the Indian and Pacific Oceans is deadly. A sting from the poisonous spines on its fins can kill a person in a few hours.

The blue whale is the largest animal that has ever lived. It can be up to 100 feet long and weigh up to 150 tons. That is as long as six elephants and as heavy as 22 elephants.

A school of whales or seals is called a pod. Killer whales go hunting in pods of up to 20 animals.

Ocean

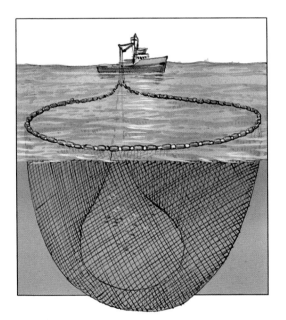

riches

⛴ Treasure from the sea

The oceans are full of treasure.
You can collect beautiful shells on the beach.

Divers find pearls inside oyster shells.

Deep down on the seafloor, there are lumps of valuable minerals. These lumps are called nodules.

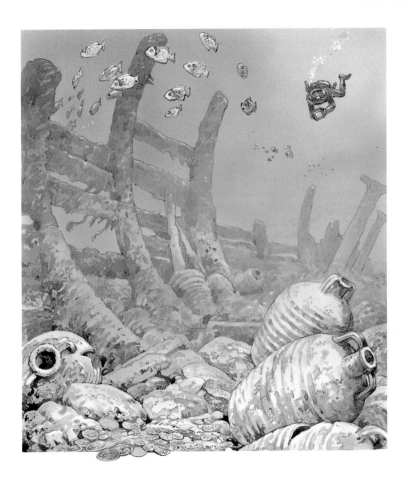

By studying shipwrecks and their cargo on the seabed, divers and scientists learn a lot about how people lived long ago.

Looking for fish

Around the world, fishermen catch more than 70 million tons of food from the sea every year.

Fishermen find fish with the help of sonar. In the ship's hull, a machine called an echo sounder sends out beeps of sound through the water. It measures the time it takes for the echoes to bounce back from the seabed. If a large school of fish gets in the way, the echo bounces back in a shorter time. The fisherman sees this on a screen.

Satellites orbiting the Earth can help too. They recognize the blue-green color of the phytoplankton that fish eat. They measure the amounts of blue and green light reflected from the ocean surface and beam pictures back to Earth. Fishermen know that where there are lots of phytoplankton there are likely to be lots of fish.

⛴ The catch

Fishermen use different nets to catch
different fish. Long drift nets hang like a
curtain from floats on the surface. Purse
seine nets trap fish in a giant net bag.
These nets catch herring, mackerel, and
other fish that swim near the surface.

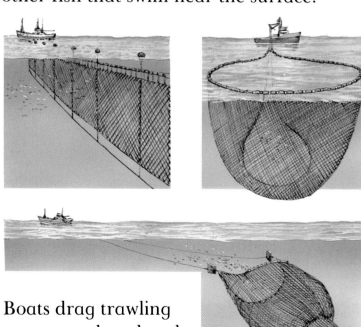

Boats drag trawling
nets to catch cod and
other fish that live
near the seabed.

The nets are hauled
in. The crew sort the
fish, clean them, and
pack them in ice to
keep them fresh.

Farming the sea

The oceans are so vast that it is easy to imagine they are a never-ending source of food. But this is not true.

Catching too many fish in one place means there are not enough fish left behind to lay eggs. And *that* means not enough fish for the future.

too many fish today...

...not enough in future

Fish farms help provide fish for the future.
At the farm, fish hatch from eggs in tanks
of water. The young fish are kept in tanks
until they are big enough to be sold and
eaten. Or they are put back into the sea.

People farm other types of seafood too,
such as mussels and edible seaweed.

mussels

seaweed

⛴ Mining the sea

One treasure from the sea is so common that we often forget about it. Everyone needs salt, and one way to get it is to use seawater.

In dry, sunny places, seawater is trapped in shallow ponds called salt pans. The heat of the sun evaporates the water, and leaves the salt behind.

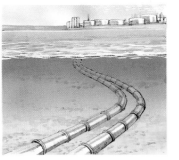

Oil and gas are buried deep beneath the seafloor. Oil rigs drill a narrow hole down to the oil and gas and pump it up to the surface. Tankers carry it all ashore, to refineries. So do underwater pipelines.

Refineries turn oil and gas into many useful products, including gasoline for cars and fuel to heat our homes.

⚓ Ocean power

Oil and gas will not last for ever, so people are looking for new sources of energy.

A power station in Norway uses waves to generate electricity. Waves push seawater up a special channel into a reservoir. The trapped water spins machines called turbines. The turbines generate electricity.

In France, engineers have built a tidal barrage across the mouth of the Rance River. Inside the barrage, turbines generate electricity when they are spun around by seawater. What happens? When the tide goes out, seawater pushes through the turbines and makes them spin. When the tide comes in, the turbines spin the other way.

Scientists and engineers are still experimenting with waves and tides.

More research will have to be done before these ideas work well enough to become useful sources of energy.

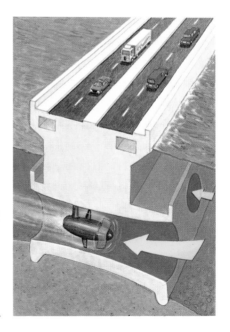

Amazing facts

Pearl divers used to hold their breath when they swam under water to collect the oysters. Most pearl divers were women, because women can stay under water longer than men without breathing. Now divers often have wet suits and tanks of air.

Lumps of copper and other precious minerals lie deep down on the seafloor. But one day it may be possible to collect these nodules.

In some hot, dry countries such as Saudi Arabia, fresh water is very scarce. Desalination is a process that removes the salt from seawater to make fresh water for people to drink.

The giant Californian kelp can grow 2 feet in one day and reaches 200 feet in length. This seaweed can provide methane gas for fuel.

People and

the sea

Studying the oceans

Oceanographers study the oceans.
They used to drop nets and simple
measuring tools over the side of a ship.

Now oceanographers can also explore the
deep with sonar. GLORIA is one echo-
sounding system. It measures sound waves
to give a clear picture of the sea floor.

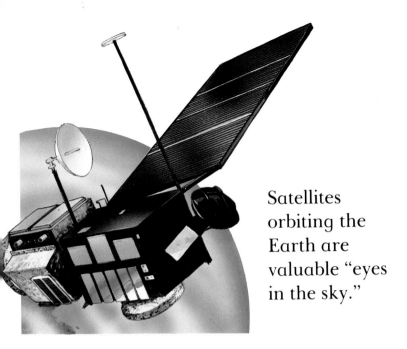

Satellites orbiting the Earth are valuable "eyes in the sky."

Satellites send out radio waves and measure how they echo off the oceans.

This gives scientists information about the shape of the seafloor, the pattern of the currents, and the temperature of the water.

 # Divers at work

Divers carry out many important building and repair jobs to underwater pipelines, cables, and oil rigs. They also explore the seabed for wrecks and wildlife.

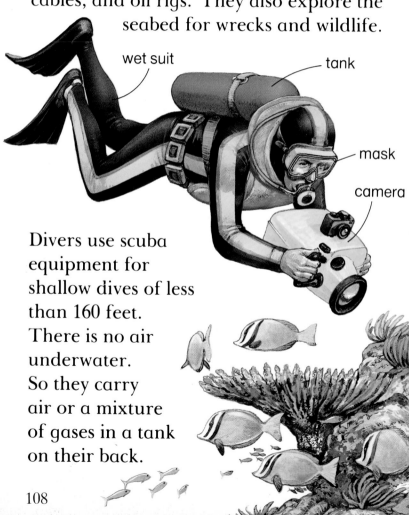

wet suit

tank

mask

camera

Divers use scuba equipment for shallow dives of less than 160 feet. There is no air underwater. So they carry air or a mixture of gases in a tank on their back.

For deeper dives, people wear diving suits made out of strong metal. Air is pumped down in a hose from a boat on the surface.

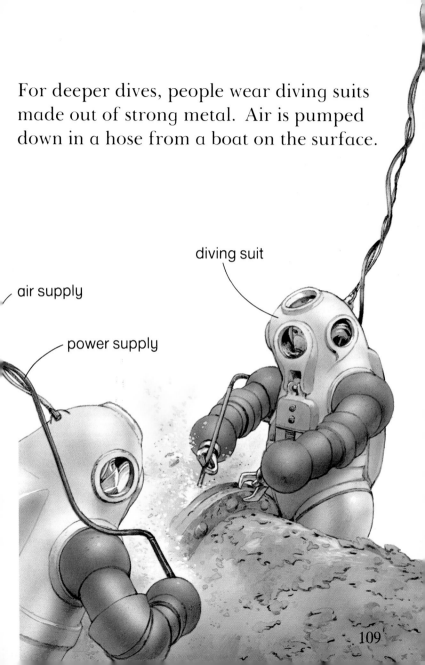

diving suit

air supply

power supply

Going down

Underwater craft called submersibles take people to the deepest parts of the ocean.

A mini-sub is launched from a ship at sea. During the trip the mini-sub crew keeps in touch with the ship. They can work underwater for up to eight hours. Then they return to the surface.

For very deep and dangerous dives, remote operated vehicles (ROVs) need no crew. They are controlled by a command cable from a support ship on the surface.

Some ROVs have robot arms that can hold cameras and tools to carry out inspections and repairs.

This ROV is scraping algae and shells off the steel legs of an oil rig.

Crossing the seas

Shipping lanes are like highways across the water for ships carrying goods from one port to another.

ferry

container ship

Different ships carry different cargo.
Huge tankers carry oil. Bulk carriers carry
grain and other dry cargo. Some ships
carry their cargo in containers. Ferries
carry people, cars, and trucks.

oil tanker

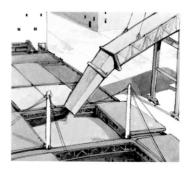

bulk carrier

Fun at the beach

The sea is a wonderful place to have fun. Lifeguards and signs tell you when it is safe to go into the water. The best beaches are clean beaches.

 # Spoiling the sea

When people dump waste into the sea, they are polluting or dirtying the water.

Pollution harms the plants and animals that live in the sea.

Some factories let poisonous waste flow into rivers and down to the sea. Farm fertilizers and pesticides also seep into the oceans. Many of them harm sea life.

Sometimes the sea is used as a garbage dump. Towns and cities pump sewage through pipelines into the sea. Barges tow garbage out to sea to get rid of it.

Oil spills from tankers can kill thousands of birds and other animals in the sea.

When the oil is washed ashore by tides and currents, it ruins our beaches too. It takes a lot of hard work to clean up the coastline after an oil spill.

Saving the sea

The oceans are beautiful, and they are valuable. Everyone should do all they can to help protect them.

Conservation groups such as Greenpeace try to protect the oceans. But there is still a lot to do.

What can you do?

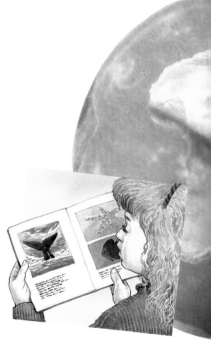

You could start by cleaning up your local beach. When you visit the seashore you could make sure you and your friends do not leave rubbish behind.

Best of all, you could learn more about the sea. Then you will know how to protect it.

Amazing facts

In 1960 two people traveled to the bottom of the deepest ocean trench, almost 7 miles down, in a submersible called a bathyscaphe.

One of the most famous research submersibles is called Alvin. In 1986 it took pictures of the Titanic, a shipwreck lying 12,000 feet below the surface in the Atlantic.

The shipping lanes around north-western Europe are very crowded. Every week ships make more than 12,000 journeys there.

In 1989 the oil tanker Exxon Valdez hit some rocks in Alaska and spilled 11 million gallons of oil. A stretch of coastline 750 miles long was covered with oil. Thousands of birds and fish were killed.

INDEX